W9-AMB-825

Tell Them It Was Mozart

Angeline
Schellenberg

Tell Them It Was
Mozart

Brick Books

Library and Archives Canada Cataloguing in Publication

Schellenberg, Angeline, 1973–, author
    Tell them it was Mozart / Angeline Schellenberg.

Poems.
Issued in print and electronic formats.
ISBN 978-1-77131-442-8 (paperback).—ISBN 978-1-77131-443-5 (epub).—
ISBN 978-1-77131-444-2 (pdf)

    I. Title.

PS8637.C4323T45 2016   C811'.6   C2016-902776-7
                                               C2016-902777-5

Copyright © Angeline Schellenberg, 2016
Second printing – November 2016

We acknowledge the Canada Council for the Arts, the Government of Canada
through the Canada Book Fund, and the Ontario Arts Council for their support of
our publishing program.

The author photo was taken by Anthony Mark Schellenberg.
The book is set in Sabon.
The cover images: Shutterstock.
Design and layout by Marijke Friesen.
Printed and bound by Sunville Printco Inc.

Brick Books
431 Boler Road, Box 20081
London, Ontario N6K 4G6

www.brickbooks.ca

for Tony,
Kieran & Gemma

Thank you for making me
a more imperfect person.

Welcome to Holland
by Emily Perl Kingsley

I am often asked to describe the experience
of rai**sing** a child **with a** disability—
to try to help people who have not sha**red** **that**
unique experience to understand it,
to imagine how it would feel. It's **like this . . .**

CONTENTS

II. It's Not What They Say

III. For Good

I. Rhythmically, in the Dark

When you're going to have a baby, it's like planning a fabulous vacation trip—to Italy. You buy a bunch of guide books and make your wonderful plans. The Coliseum. The Michelangelo David

1980 El Camino

Kennelled in the hindquarters
of that mongrel car-truck,
brother and I roll
with Dad's sharp turns,
Chef Boyardee cans, and dust,
caged in fibreglass and frayed
rug, unable to sit upright,
tapping glass with tiny fingers
Mom and Dad ignore
in favour of the sick baby
filling the plush seat
between them.

Brother flaps hands, licks lips,
stares me down
like I'm the fly caught
in the sliding window
where my lips press the screen for air
and I'm praying
for Jesus to leap
from the Life is Precious sign
and save us from this
Tuesday errand.
Save us from each other.

X

Fragile X is the most common form

of inherited mental delay and the leading known

cause of autism, the result of a mutation of a single gene

isolated in 1991 (like a sister leaving home)

on the long arm of the X chromosome

(that my great-grandma passed to

my grandpa passed to

my mom passed to

my brothers

(and me?)),

a mutation that prevents the production of a protein

(not listed on the Frosted Flakes box)

vital for brain development.

If the DNA strand extends slightly beyond the normal

length of six to forty-four repeats, it's called a premutation, and

that man or woman will

(like my great-grandma

and grandpa

and mom

(and me?))

become an unaffected

carrier of a gene prone to further expansion when passed

in future generations from mother to child, reaching beyond

two hundred repeats (the number of times my brother

made me watch *Annie*),

4

stretching so thin that it shuts down (faster than

the Avro Arrow), giving the chromosome

a pinched appearance

(like the cuffs on our matching long johns).

Boys with the full mutation are more severely impacted than girls who

have a second healthy X from the other parent

to compensate. Eighty-four percent of affected boys have attention

deficit, seventy percent have anxiety, sixty-six percent are hyperactive,

forty-six percent have autism,

forty-one percent self-injure, thirty-eight percent experience aggression

(my brother won in every category,

including powerlifting and relay). Expect

swollen adenoids due to a unique facial structure

(forcing my baby brother to fight for breath in the night, exposing his ribs,

distending his belly like the starving children on the fridge—leading

the pediatrician to accuse our mom of neglect). One in every

259 women carries Fragile X and has a one in two chance of

passing it on to each child because

she has one X from each of her parents to offer,

and (no matter how great a nurse my mom was and how hard she prayed

for her children to have any health problem

but an invisible one), a mother's body

chooses at random

where to place each

X.

The Hopes and Fears of All the Years

It was the Christmas letters my parents dreaded most
the year my brother's hyperactivity was assessed
and the baby almost stopped breathing in his sleep
—circulars spun full of family camping trips,
soccer goals, piano solos, chess championships.
They fell, heat-seeking missives, throughout December
onto our kitchen table, to be read after dark,
returned to like tongues
to cavities. If I'd dared to write it,
our letter would've read:
The little one makes us gasp,
his brother keeps us busy, and
our first-born has done little
worth noticing.

Our Garden of Thorns

Useless blue-green vegetable,
prickly lettuce grew on either side
of our shortcut home,
bled bitter milk, flung seeds
into the future.

Your kicked-up gravel dust
caked our noses as we straddled
our ditch bridge, and I cultivated names
for those foetid flowers, thorny
as the question:

how many know our secret,
that what appears soft (when
looked down upon)
may be sharp as your mind
to those who move close enough
to touch?

Remember how I'd stumble Chaplin-style
into the prickly patches, feign
surprise at their sting, just to hear
you laugh? Little brother,
I'd sacrifice both shins for you.

You told me I'd go away
to grow a family, while you'd stay
and grow white like Opa, like Santa,
like the downy achenes
that settled beneath our feet.

In our garden of thorns,
we sat till soporific heat
became our salve,
the wild lettuce turning
leaf margins to the sun, a living
compass along our path, pointing us
toward home. And away.

The Test

Circle *no*
to genetic certainty.
Become the black hole
on a Fragile X researcher's diagram,
the red question mark on your family tree.

Or: check *yes*
to the bloody smears
that may mark half your eggs
as bearing stretched genes: delayed milestones, large ears,
long faces.

Consider this case study: would the cute boys
leaning strong hands
on your college canteen counter
ask you out for coffee
if they knew you had
a 50/50 chance?

Clue

I was scratching mustard from my scarlet slacks at the microfiche when
you and your friend came in and taped me to my chair. He left,

you stayed to get me unstuck.

You hummed an Italian love song and told me about the girl:
how you never got the nerve to kiss her, how she never asked

why not?

I said the artist in biology doesn't know my name. I just want
someone to notice. (I just want someone to kiss.)

You said, yes, someone who'll listen, someone I can sing to,
a girl who makes me brave.

In a second's silence
I felt the jolt as it flashed across your face:

why not you and me?

Now, I tell everyone about the moment I got a clue:
it was the music major, in the library, with the masking tape.

Freshman Reading

In biology: defects.

In psych: disorders.

In theology: even the risen Christ has wounds.

In the Fragile X geneticist's letter,
a guarantee: my kids will be *perfect*.

Family Ties

Every day after school, I turned
on the TV and spent time
with my family: Mom, Dad,
Alex, Mallory, Jennifer, and Andy.
There weren't no nothing
we couldn't love each other through.

The first time you
brought me home to loud turkey
dinners, your brothers' bad
puns, your sisters' hugs, your mom
patting my behind,
the show went on and on.

I stood in the aisle
while you sang forever love.
My parents said their line
to give me away,
and I stepped onto the stage
in a princess gown,
ready.

rail coach

the train ran
right by our first
apartment   loco-
motives coupled

freight
from down the line
rolling over your next
thought like a penny

rattling
our fish bowl   catching
us off guard like rent

waking
us at three to that horn plenty of
times

steeling us for the future

heavy things
come   and   go   but

this spirit stays

any blow
can be a call to pray

Ultrasound

The heart monitor
pointed at my uterus
picks up only static from
a hostile planet.

Like four years ago.
The tech can't find anything of
consequence through my belly.

No point in my husband missing his finals just to hear
the doctor will be in touch (to set the date to scrape me
clean). Nothing to see but me holding
my bladder. Holding
my breath. The tech guarding a dark screen.

She must probe me
for signs. She presses my vagina here. And
here. Clicks.

And turns the screen to
face me.

There you are.

A tiny twig
bursting into bud. No:
those are fingers and toes.
You wave first.

The tech measures your
kicking legs from knee
to toe. You weren't hiding—
you're just too small to send
your heartbeat
echoing through my shell.

Oh, my stick figure, glowing
on my lids when I close my eyes.
Very soon you will leap
off this screen.

labour

headless human torso possessed by darkness
and Demerol, everything below the ribs shaken
loose   hips, amniotic fluid, dignity   daydreams
bursting with blood and fresh-cut jewels

punctured thigh, glow and itch, electric
sparks up pinched hip nerve   wires crossed
tightening noose of heart monitor strap
to slice a body into two

hypnotizing pulse, beating waves
radio transmission from inner space, alien
uterine tsunami sucking out to sea

speeding train   trapped between metallic mouth
and pelvis   pounded, jagged plow   ram/
reverse/re-rail to bust a board   throb
see how long this pubic bone can hold

rhythmic retching bursts
pumpkin flesh open, vagina flipped
inside-out   a tube sock
puppet sewn up with eyes
Xs and Os in invisible places

It's a Boy

Complete this sentence: *As long as it's healthy* . . .

By the time your own startle reflex has kicked in
and he's tested his grasp of your finger,
melting your belly from the outside,

you'll have counted his toes, one to ten, twice—
as if there's something to do with missing toes
—searched his frosted eyes, scried his tears,

pressed his belly, pressed the nurse
for assurance that, unlike your brothers,
he will someday write his name, hug you back.

As you pour yourself into him at three a.m. . . . .
stare out the glazed window,
rock rhythmically in the dark.

While You Churned

While you churned inside,
I dreamed you slipped
from between my buttered thighs,
leapt like a calf from my bed.
You danced around the edges
of the room, tore cords
from every hospital wall,
oblivious to the oxygen-hooked—
you laughed at connections.
My heavy arms
too slow to hold you.

When you entered the room
with your face to the sun
(your skull, pressed into my spine,
had cut off my nerve) and
they set you on my belly,
your arms and legs opened
like an old sock monkey.
I held you eight months
till you pulled your teeth back
from my breast
and ran away, your shock
of hair not even high enough
to brush the table.
My gravity
too weak to capture you.

I was never diagnosed

unless you count the morning the nurse—immune all night to my
depressed button after dumping a newborn in my lap at two a.m. with no
bassinette to lay him down in and leaving me (no strength in my arms to
carry him) dozing upright, humming in fluorescent light through woozy
nightmares of tossing waves and fears of smothering—came to tell me: *No,
it's another hour till breakfast* ... then

I cried

and the nurse brought me
a social worker (I *wanted*
toast) to warm my hand, cup
my cheek, and say
no matter how sad I felt,
not to hold my baby

under the bathwater,
and every nurse afterward
checked my chart, shook
her head, and clucked:
postpartum.

Years later, when sadness swallows
me till I can't feel my own tongue,
I tell no one—knowing the stickiness
of charts, fearing the social worker
I've drowned out
may resurface.

The Nature of Nurture

Here's what I remember:
holding him close, stroking nectarine
cheeks, the curls of his ear, his bright
pupils searching mine as I
trickled sweet milk and stress
hormones into his contracting
belly, fulfilling dire checkout
stand predictions, freezing
his fragile neurons
with every anxious
drop.

My Undoing

Cupboards that won't lock, that spill knives
and pills into your fumbling hands,

my boy, the way you slip from my grasp to play
on banisters, in headlights,

the sleep-deprived vigilance that keeps me thinking
there must be two or three of you,

the cackle that sends you thumping into the hall mirror, spinning
Red Devil lure, making my own arms ache,

the lie that whispers, *Just one slap would
snap you out of it.*

Watching Him Sleep 1

Now I lay me down . . .

Rest your head on the crib bars,
blow his downy hair.
Watch his cowlick fall.

This one's a keeper, the nurse said.

You can't beg for forgiveness
from one who can't speak.

Just love him, the pastor said.

The Runaway Housewife at One a.m.

Leave your husband and son, travel west
over the tomato vomit in the hallway, toward
a ghost town—say Sanctuary, Saskatchewan,
with a possible overnight in Hyde. First, find
the door. Grab the last cinnamon bun:
to dull the razor blade of your tongue. Listen
a moment to the *clink-clock* of your hot buttons
tumbling in the dryer. The Ikea in your mind
may yet have an exit. Stare past the Velcro
voices, the selvages you've managed to unravel.
There is no sin in the stumble to surrender. Falling
feels like the dog's muzzle between the sofa cushions,
and tonight, the last flush is your amen.

When I Knew I Loved You

They said it would be love
at first sight, but you look
nothing like my father, your dad, or
the child I thought of when I said your name.

I feel the letdown
of milk and warmth from heart
to nipple. I watch your navel rise.

I stroke the ear that's closest,
the wax, the down.
I will your hair to grow.

I peel off your diaper and marvel
at manhood in miniature, the mess
in a million wrinkles.

A second pregnancy,
a new fluttering
beneath my heart, but
I'm too caught up in your
lost shoe, stuck zipper
to wonder.

She emerges head first,
and love is a flash because

she looks just like you.

Interior Lighting

Hospital rooms are bright for a reason:
through me, she entered one
as a small Sol
flaring round and infrared,
glossed and quivering,
      too radiant
for the naked eye.

When the doctor placed her
face up on my harrowed belly,
her arms flew open—
like an inverted beetle,
a wind-washed daisy,
      like my own gaping
ultraviolet awe.

Your First Year

The shadow of a body, an impression
on my breast as I chase your brother
through parks, change his diapers,
suspect something,
mix his milk with oatmeal
and tears, you, always
filling my arms—
a warm, empty belly
without a face.

Crossing that Bridge

Imagine this: you're driving
across an ice-black bridge
for the first time as a mother of two;
your right hand grips the wheel,

barely hanging on, your ragged breath
catches on the question: if

you should fly over the edge, sink
into sepia, undo restraints meant to save them . . .

before you're all three sucked under, swirling,

when you've broken
free of all that's solid,

look down,

which child are your arms holding:

the one who needs you most?
the one you've loved the longest?
the one you haven't damaged
yet?

The Diminutive Professor Takes Off

The sofa cushions never stay where I put them:
they slide into the hall, line up along the wall,
take flight to worlds the Wright brothers never dreamed—

with one push of a Lego button, you're up and away,
where bristling toothbrushes can't reach,
even Cassiopeia doesn't have to stay in her seat,
whining fluorescents lose their power.
Your mom's eyes, a distant memory.

Rattling on about weather, dodging meteors,
blocking my path to the kitchen,
three-year-old pilot,
slight as star tail,
lost in space.

Purple Squirrel!

Breathe a word about those mauve mammals—perhaps
there are three outside your window now—and
your dad will feign fear, his voice squeak *where?*
where? his hands trembling at the wheel
while you throw your head back
and giggle.

When we're not there yet,
when socks are soaked,
when seatbelts pinch,
and every Hangman has hung,
when Dad has just about had it
and all juice is gone,

purple squirrels leap
from corn stalks and trash bins
to surf passing cars and swing from power lines.

Grey or brown
or even aquamarine rodents
are fair game for stray dogs,
but the purple ones, ah,
their googly eyes are winking
just for us.

The Runaway Housewife at Two p.m.

You consider leaving them
on the preschool teacher's porch
like orphans. She has all the answers
and you have nothing left
but black bananas. Your mom can make them
stop crying, but you can't even stop
yourself, so you dream you're running
as far as paralyzed legs can carry you
to bury your face under another mother's
pillow and seep away into her mattress
like sweat. You hold open your front door and
watch yourself tumble
down concrete steps
to land in sweet unresponsiveness
       for just one night.

your greatest fear

watch your step
bringing in the mail   if
you lose   your balance
and slip
he will not   *bring mommy the phone*   *sweetie*
or stroke your hair
crying
wake up mommy mommy wake up—

he will laugh
                a prisoner finally
free
and the gate will flap like
torn skin
                behind him

Vaccination

An injection for every disease,
but for guilt, no immunity.

How many mothers
sprayed paint in the first trimester?
Martha Stewart taught me how
to make Christmas wrap
from newspapers: silver mist
was your swaddling cloth.

I scrubbed tiles with CLR,
swapped Mozart for McGraw,
stepped on doused dandelions,
and what about the tuna?

I'm weeping over
your Sharpie swirls,
while you poke my face
and yell, *Hey juice!*
In this moment,
both of us resistant

to every known strain
of empathy.

Watching Him Sleep 2

I'm sorry I can't let your imagination run
wild into every puddle and pile of
pasta. I'm sorry I think *what if* and
someday.

There is no way
to make you mind without
losing mine. I'm sorry
I can't choose.

I'm sorry I took you to
the post office. I'm sorry I couldn't buy every
sympathy card you sent flying. I'm sorry
I heard what they whispered
behind our backs.

I'm sorry—
when you jumped
onto the sofa and knocked the empty
picture frame
onto your sleeping
sister's fragile skull—
that for just one second,
I loved her better.

Echolalia (the Monologue)

be be be be   see see see

I'd like to buy an eye?
Sorry, there are no eyes.

Stimulate your senses.
Feel what it's like to chew 5.
Cooling, warming, tingling sensations
on the tongue.

Are you thirsty, honey?
Are you thirsty, honey?
Are you thirsty, honey?

mm mmm
Not from concentrate.
No wonder it tastes so good!

Uh oh! Squawk! Look what you've done!

Coming up on the Nature Channel: parrots
that can speak a hundred words in proper context.
Training requires a great deal of patience!

Well, talk to me! Squawk!

o o o o!   y y y?

When will your dad be home!
When will your dad be home!
When will your dad be home!

Now removes three times more grime with every swipe!
Ten more fragrances your mom will love!

I'd like to buy an eye?
Sorry, there are no eyes.

No one can stop Robot Zot!
Robot Zot conquer all!
Robot Zot never fall!

Come here, honey.
Come here, honey.
Come here, honey.

u u u!

I'd like to buy a you?
Yes, there is one you.

The Imaginative Child Takes a Bath

We cannot keep the bathroom empty enough for your exploratory hands.
How you squirt and spread yourself thick and thin!
I see the vanishing cream has disappeared for good,
and a potion of makeup removers has transported you to a far-off pool
Mary Kay never imagined, seething with Pert shampoo.
Streaks of Anusol slip into your scratches.
Hello, here's a design clipped into your brows.
Droplets bead on your lipsticked lids.
Frothy arms shaved clean, toenails bloodied—
looks like you've gone and had a hazing, my tenderfoot.
Go, camouflage your flawless hide in PJs
while I settle myself in your puddles and drain
the rainbows from the tub.
The left side of what was once your
chin-length bob floats free and
clings to the curtain.

The Diminutive Professor Visits the Duck Pond

He says nothing, just walks off the path around the pond, squats in the mud, and starts to dig.

He doesn't look up when geese land in the water, folding in their wings beside him. He gathers sticks and stones, lays them down in neat rows. Adds a layer, and another, criss-crosses. Lovingly, he smooths mud over the sides, the top.

Stroller-pushers steer clear of his mess. They look for a mom to explain these unwashed fingers. To make sense of why he is here.

Coming closer, I realize he's been singing, *Here by the water, I'll build an altar to praise Him out of the stones that I've found here. I'll set them down here, rough as they are. Knowing You can make them holy.*

A song we heard once, at a church where I wept, wondering if he'd ever listen.

When his work is finished, my dry hand will reach for his. We will meander home together to get clean. He will lead the way.

Saints

Saint Ciaran knew
God before God's name
was heard in Ireland. He didn't save
the day like Patrick, but when he prayed,
the hawks and badgers knelt down
at his feet.

I named you after Ciaran
so you'd draw in wonder, sense
mysteries you wouldn't hear in my
anxious breaths.

Saint Gemma was a wild
soul wanting the wounds
of her Saviour; for evidence
of love, praying to feel his pain.

My Gem, you're a wired one,
tossing Bibles, asking Jesus—
if he's there—to catch them,
biting fingers raw to let the ache
in your blood flow free.

I am no saint or angel.
Like Eve I bequeath you
the thorns, the birds, my fear
for which there is no name.

Pain Threshold

I knew the moment I caught you strumming
the rusted vent cover, making musical notes
sharp enough to slice baby fingers to shreds,
your ear tuned only to the harp of your own making,
my neck tingling with the pain you could not feel.
Florid thrums fill in the gaps with red. Resonate.

II. It's Not What They Say

But there's been a change in the flight plan.
They've landed in Holland and there you must stay.
The important thing is that they haven't taken you to a horrible,
disgusting, filthy place, full of pestilence, famine and disease.

The Diminutive Professor Takes a Walk

Those perennials are photosynthesizing to create glucose as food for the plant, you announce on the way to kindergarten. The weeding neighbour looks up and stares, but you, my five-year-old botanist, only have eyes for her sedums.

We'll be late if you keep rescuing elm saplings wedged between sidewalk blocks, tossing acorns down manholes to calculate the distance between us and all that rushes underneath. I hold tight to keep you from darting to the next igneous, sedimentary, or metamorphic rock across the street.

In your backpack, a Crayola diagram of a leaf's cell structure—it's your day for sharing. Last week, it was the digestive system. You returned, amazed how many kids weren't aware of their villi. Even now, they're waving nutrients into our bloodstreams—like flicking fingers. Like the tiny fingers wriggling out of my hand.

Cycle-ogy 1

for example does your child ever line up blocks for hours
spin toy car wheels instead of driving them
scream over seams
repeat everything you say
line up blocks spin wheels instead of
for example eat olives every breakfast repeat
everything you say line up
blocks of hours spin
toy car wheels on his cheeks instead of
fall in love with sticks
for example throw himself into walls
cry when you laugh
repeat
everything
you say line up
block
spin
repeat

everything you say

The Little Hand Is at the One

The shrink's desk clock ticks off the reasons
you should not have had children:

You can't help them.
You almost lost them.
You cry all day long.

Wait for judgments like zippers
to snag your resolve.

What to take to prove yourself?
Attachment classes,
Positive Parenting pamphlets,
your chances.

Her glossy lips ask
what's going on at home:

Away at work more? (They need you home.)
Going out with friends less? (You need support.)
You and your husband fight?

Each gesture,
every word whispered here
is professionally assessed
for nuance:

The way you choke *If*—desperation.

The way you stare at her locking file drawer—fear.

The way you hold your hand in your lap—a sure
sign of surrender.

Why I Am Honest with the Therapist about
My Part-Time Job, Waffle Makers, and Bon Jovi

We will respect the client's privacy and confidentiality except
in cases where we believe the client
to be at risk of willful self-injury or suicide.

I have read and understood the above.

You Must Believe in Life after Yesterday

Because the Canada goose craps green, holds its head high, and mates for life.

Because twenty-seven million new doughnuts enter the world daily.

Because you can't count the hairs that slip from your head to catch in trees.

Because there are infinite shades of blue, and some of them are electric.

You've never tasted cheese made from the milk of Balkan donkeys.

The crickets can fill in any silence.

The fridge magnet poking out of the baseboard says *elaborate*.

Hope holds its china cup high in your mind and pours.

The hummingbird remembers every flower.

Sleep is your favourite flannel shirt, fish taking flight between the buttons.

Someday you'll find yourself where all is water and thirst.

Your thoughts fall as petals into an open palm.

You don't know what the turtles hum while you sleep.

Because God is the golden eagle nest on every ledge.

Because death is a dream in which no one is chasing you.

Because the wind circles you. Turns your hair into a compass.

Certainty

The principal holding
your psych assessment asks,
Why didn't you tell us
Fragile X
runs in your family?
(Implied: *Why didn't you avoid*
the risk, choose to adopt,
have a tubal?)

How can I make
her understand that the one thing,
the only thing, of which
I've learned I can be certain
is exactly how far
the gene she's pointing to (at position Xq27.3)
could have stretched?

Everything else,
from your eye colour to
your flight obsession,
is a crapshoot,
an extravagant mystery.

Cycle-ogy 2

early intervention is key
but he looks fine to me
try ignoring the behaviour   come back in a year
the waiting list is ten to twelve months   we'll call you
he's too young for diagnosis   come back in a year   try natural
consequences   come back in a year   the waiting list is twelve to eighteen
months   we'll call you   why aren't you using time outs   come back next
week   watch this 1-2-3 Magic video   try this workbook   come in
I'm sorry
he's too old for our program
why didn't you seek
help sooner
haven't you
heard early
intervention
is key?

I Am a Refrigerator Mother

There is no raid shelter from the verbal bombs that rain on
contemporary parents. —Leo Kanner, 1941

1.

"Autism" comes from the Greek *autos* for "self" and *ismos* for "state of
being."

They are who they are.

2.

The refrigerator mother theory traces back to Leo Kanner—the first to
identify autism as a separate condition in 1943 and author of *Folklore of
the Teeth*—who claimed autism is caused by mothers "just happening to
defrost enough to produce a child."

I am listening to another shrink diagnose
my boy with a soft disciplinarian,
my girl with a weak mother-child bond.

3.

Bruno Bettelheim was a doctor of art history, a fairy-tale scholar making
believe he was a psychologist with all the fanfare of Oz.

A concentration camp survivor, Bettelheim decided the autistic child
disappeared inside like a Nazi torture victim. Like a child whose mother
wanted him dead.

Bettelheim told parents *Love is Not Enough*. Popularizing Leo Kanner's icy
form of blame, he gave the world *Symbolic Wounds*, *The Empty Fortress*.

When sticky fingers pull on me,
I light up and swing open.

Take that, Leo.

Clone

Someday the nature/nurture people will clone you. They will place new
you in the perfect home. They will prepare new mother for everything.
She will not scream when you don't respond to your name. She will have
the best cognitive behavioural therapists on hold. She will have no desire
to escape into blogs or to smoother shorelines in her mind. She will never
be surprised. She will know when to ask you sweetly to use your fork and
when to join you on the chair in praise to Bob the Tomato. She'll never
mistake your anxious laughs for defiance, your tipping chairs for hate.
She will not bite Os into her arms for remorse or bang her head on door
frames. She will never weep beside your bed or pray for mercy. Each night
her team will debrief her as they rub her feet, her back, her frozen smile.
She will know this is only an experiment.

Beyond Words

There is the nun
who holds my question
in her cupped palms like a chalice. Waits
for me to breathe.

There is a cat.
My empty lap. My gentle *come*.
She slides her fur across the edge
of my hem. Lets me feel
the hollow of her belly. Chooses
not to leap.

There is my son.
His soft *I don't know*. The book
between us. His head almost
touching mine on the pillow.

We Leave with a Label

Something's wrong: my kid is always happy!

When the ice cream slipped off his cone, he said, "Oh well, next time." He grins for time outs, giggles at pain.

Outside the one-way mirror: "Dr. Aspie," the psychiatrist who confirms suspicions.

I reach for my son, but this book has no words. I describe the pictures, fight to put enough emotion into my voice to hold him beside me. To prove to the other side of the glass that a lack of love is not the reason we are here.

Dr. Aspie enters and asks him to name his best friend, his favourite food on earth. My son whirls around our chairs, a helicopter of words and giggles: *All propulsion systems at maximum!*

He always this oblivious? Dr. Aspie wants to know. My son still spinning, the psychiatrist turns to me and does his best impression of a flight attendant:

Welcome to Aspergers.

Absorbed

The year before my father was born, Hans Asperger noticed difficulties with social skills in children with typical intelligence and language—whom he called "the little professors."

Aspergers entered the psychiatric Bible the year I married your dad—proof of the existence of "just a dash of autism."

I heard of Aspergers at the end of your first grade—after years of hearing you were "too bright/talkative/engaged" for a diagnosis.

I heard of Aspergers just seven years before Aspergers was deleted—absorbed under the umbrella of the autism spectrum.

Aspergers' short life as a condition
was enough time to explain to me
why you went from loving
cell division at age four to
pipe organs at seven
without ever holding my hand.

Autism for Dummies 1

1.
somebody somewhere
beyond the silence

at home in the land of Oz

exiting Nirvana
under the banana moon

a tunnel of hope
a spiral down
the rabbit hole

unstrange minds remapping the world

2.
     girl in the panda hat
     horse boy
a free-range Aspergian
the invisible cage

one bite at a time
the dog-eat-dog world
decoding brains trains and video games
beating the odds
     the boy who loved windows
     the girl who loved cows

experts
targeting autism
from the garden of Eden to the parting of the Red Sea

send in the idiots
who said autistic children can't learn
hello my name is
    cruel blessing
    homesick alien

welcome to
life behind glass

everyone pretend to be normal

The Other You

Dear brother, I saw him again the other day
at the shoe store, the pizza place, the park.
Uncanny: that same strong jaw,
long nose, brush cut.
In a booth full of friends,
playing air guitar,
ordering a personal pizza.
(He's not afraid to say what he likes
in cheese, music, women.)
There he is, throwing that football far and wide,
laughing when he's tackled on the sand,
car keys and promise ring in his pack,
college acceptance letter in the mail.
I imagine walking over, calling out, *Hey*,
imagine he turns and grins and says,
There you are—because
he is you, baby brother,
with one more neural protein.
Or maybe just one less damaged
message about
what he is
capable of.

Drug Trial

Call to the stand
the mother.

Disorder
is in the court.

Evidence:
the holes in her appearance,
her son's flight from every scene,
his statements repeating
for the record.

He did
exhibit a
range of unusual behaviours
on the days and nights
in question.

Recall the forceps, the vaccines,
her obvious admission of guilt.

Her burden is proof.

You will judge
for yourself how well she's doing.

Cycle-ogy 3

Strattera resolves hyperactivity causes depression
Prozac addresses depression releases aggressiveness
Risperdal arrests aggression adds weight Strattera
resolves hyperactivity causes depression Prozac
addresses depression releases aggressiveness Risperdal
arrests aggression adds weight Strattera resolves
hyperactivity causes depression Prozac addresses
depression releases aggressiveness Risperdal arrests
aggression adds weight Strattera resolves hyperactivity
causes depression Prozac addresses depression
releases aggressiveness Risperdal arrests aggression
adds weight Strattera resolves hyperactivity causes
depression Prozac addresses depression releases
aggressiveness Risperdal arrests aggression adds
tics

What Doctors Took Seven Years to Discover

He sits cross-legged on the sofa.

In his lap, a library book about Amazing Alphie,

a little computer wired

differently from all the others. Yelled at.

Laughed at. Saves the day.

A tear slides down my boy's lip,

but his eyes are calm. *I'm Alphie*, he says.

Relieved this feeling finally has a name.

DSM-5: Aphorism Speculum Disorder (ASD)

Diagnostic criteria:

A. Persistent deficits in social commotion and socket interceptors across multiple continental breakfasts, as manifested by the folly, curiously or by histrionics:

1. Deficits in social-emotional reciprocating engines, ranging, for example, from abnormal sock approval and failure of normal back-and-forth convertibles; to reduced sharing of infests, emollients, or Affenpinschers; to failure to initiate or respond to social Darwinist interference.

2. Deficits in non-veranda communicative beefeaters used for sock-eye interbreeding, randomizing, for exaggeration, from poorly integrated verboten and non-vintage communalism; to abnormalities in eye cream and boogie language or deficits in understanding and use of jesters; to a total lack of facial espresso and non-volatile commuters.

3. Deficits in developing, maintaining, and understanding relatives, ranching, for excavation, from difficulties adjusting beholders to suit various so-called contests; to difficulties in sharing imaginative playwrights or in making fridges; to the abscess of interims in pears.

B. Restricted, repetitive pattering of belabourers, interest groups, or acts of God, as manifested by at least two of the followers, cursively or by hysterectomy (exasperations are illusory, not exhibitionist; see texture):

1. Stereotyped or repetitive motor mauve mints, use of object lessons, or speedways (for exactitude, simple motorized stereoscopes, lining up toy poodles or flipping obelisks, echolocation, idiosyncratic phasers).

2. Insistence on same nest, inflexible adherence to Roots tees, or ritualized pastures of verbena or non-verbose bee-haters (for exacerbation, extreme distress at small changelings, difficulties with transit, rigid thinking patroons, greeting rickshaws, need to take sane router or eat safe fools every daydream).

3. Highly restricted, fixated internets that are abnormal in insectary or folkdance (for Excalibur, strong attaché case to or pre-puberty with unusual objections, excessively circumstellar or perseverative interstates).

4. Hyper- or hypo-reactivity to sensory ingot or unusual intersections in sensory aspirates of the envelop (for exception, apparent indigenousness to pang/tempest, adverse repose to specific soups or Texans, excessive smelling or tousling of oboes, visual fascination with lignocellulose or moussaka).

Specify current severity:

Waving

Some days, all we crave is
something that waves back.

The flags at the fairground hold out
arms of surrender. Now we understand the monarch

on wind-whipped willow boughs, tugging
at our ache with each wingbeat, our ears tuned

to the song of the furious washerwoman
flapping silk knits. The school bus swings

a red harbinger of homecomings into our path. At the end
of my rope, my dog waves her tail in welcome,

mirroring the arms of other people's children.

We Leave with a Sticker Chart

Something's wrong: my kid is always angry!

When the ice cream slipped off her cone, she threw her boot at my head.

Beside me on the sofa, "Dr. Brush-off," the psychiatrist famous for
denying anything is wrong.

I list the McDonald's treats she won't touch, the kid she decked for not
believing in fairies, the fact that she won't wear pants.

To prove to Dr. Brush-off that a lazy grab for disability tax credits is not the
reason we are here, I rub my daughter's elbow, expecting her to scream.

But today she's too busy sketching medieval weapons to notice.

Support Group I

We stare at sample schedules and fill the margins with doodles of exploding houses.

We hold up stories like broken playthings: the school that ordered Medicated Barbie, the Child and Family Services G.I. Joe.

We finger a rosary of failures in our pockets.

The fluorescent light carries a tune we've learned to hum.

We clutch bags filled with earplugs and smooth stones.

We wait for someone to bring up Prozac and slide to the edge of common sense.

We gnaw the insides of our cheeks.

We play one-downmanship games for tokens of pity:

> children who may never say *I love you,*
> teens able to say *I want to die,*
> bolters before tires that won't stop squealing in our sleep.

We wear our disillusionments like cloaking devices.

We don't make eye contact.

The Diminutive Professor Takes Summer Vacation

I need a welding kit, he tells me, his training wheels wobbling. *What do you think of the axial catwalk?* he asks and holds plans up to my face, crew's quarters and passenger decks neatly labelled squares on the back of his report card. *And sheet metal. Lots of canvas.*

Can't brush his teeth without a stool, but this kid's got environmentally friendly air travel in the bag. He assures me the prototype's scale model will fit between the barbeque and sandbox. And bracing wires. He'll need bracing wires.

On the way home, a stop for ice cream cones, library books on flight. *The Hindenburg should have waited for helium,* he says. *They used the accessible hydrogen, but it's far more flammable. They shouldn't have been in such a hurry to take off.*

Autism for Dummies 2

1.
why I take vitamins
        mother warriors

twirling naked in the streets and no one noticed
bright splinters of the mind

I'm no Mother Teresa

a nation of parents
embracing
trains tractors and high explosives
whole-body strategies for
waging war on
        the panic virus
        trampolines and bouncy castles
        eye-locks and other fearsome things

to puberty and beyond
guns a-blazing

2.
accidental teacher
miraculous child
through the eyes of aliens
finding me
        land we can share
        a dog and a prescription for laughter

how could you manage
how autism changed
how to be human

The "Building Blocks of Attachment" Program

We must go on camera
in a dark room
to prove I love you.

The doctors will channel Freud.
They will ask about your delivery
and my mother. Collect my tissues.

They will tell us
to build our wooden towers,
watch them fall.

They will tape our connection
so they can go back over it,
pause us, pencils poised.

It's Not What They Say

It's just quirkiness, your toe walk to whimsy.
It's put on, like a satin dress in the sandbox.
It's a sign of intelligence, your four-syllable words for *no*.
It's the thrash of alligator arms that won't be shoved into a sweater.
It's poor parenting. It's just attention-seeking, your screams over
lumpy jelly, it's the brother's example, the way he gulps hysteria like
helium, it's poor parenting it's the food colouring turning your lips blue
your brain to slush it's poor parenting it's time for meds a side effect of
my inattention it's the teacher immune to the tingly coolness
of brick and the slip of pudding it's poor parenting it's forever
it's not fair that in twenty years my friends' festive tables
will grow leaves. It's poor parenting. It's my fault,
the way I unhinge like an old refrigerator.
It's story time, tucked into tattered quilts,
you and me and our talking mice.
It's the smell of your hair,
like falling oranges and hosed dog.
It's still you.

The Imaginative Child Contemplates a Drug Bust

My daughter is convinced the police are coming. She holds up the drawstring bag she found last week in my night table drawer. White lumps. Just like the ones the German shepherds sniffed out on TV.

She's been waiting for the knock at the door, the handcuffs.
Afraid to ask *when*.

I untie the string and pop a dusty rock into my mouth, breathe on her cheek. Not the sting of mint, not the handwritten tag—*Thanks for sharing our special day*—can convince her.

She's torn between hiding under the bed and calling 911. She can't imagine what it will feel like to fall asleep without a mother.

What I Told the School Division Bigwig in My Head after the Meeting

He's not deaf. He hears

everything you

see—fluorescent lights exciting

mercury vapour in a high-intensity

reaction, the classroom door as it screams

open, the teacher's soles on cold

tile, the wall clock counting

down the seconds till she

notices his pen not

moving. Her breath

on his neck.

High

You've got that early morning pre-Ritalin buzz
like you've both been sucking sufficient helium
to raise the dead, with screeches high enough to wake owls
and send the neighbours' tents packing. Golly,
it'll take a hostage mediator with a bullhorn
just to find out what you want for breakfast.
Your broken record's needle skips on inside jokes
about slugs in socks and Vader's potatoes,
punchlines whacking my eardrums till they thump a solo,
your eyes twinkling with Martian mischief.
May I borrow a gasp of this laughing gas,
just to see me through till nine,
when your opiates peak and
bring you down to earth again?

Echolalia (the Sibling Dialogue)

If anyone in my kingdom is found to be a king,
he shall be taken to jail and turned into a fat pizza guy.

Signed, the king.

If anyone in my kingdom is found to own less than three hundred wolves,
he shall be taken to jail and be eaten by wolves.

Signed, the king.

Crinkle, crinkle, little two-headed bunnies. How I wonder what you are!

How I wonder what you are!

What you are!

Great wholesome crunchy goodness!

Great bursts of tiny flavoured crystals!

Rotten eggs with eye patches!

There are a thousand fighter jets on my back.

I'm off to our secret lab.

I'm off to find potatoes!

Vader's potatoes. My Spidey sense is tingling!

Great bursts of tiny flavoured crystals!

Great wholesome crunchy goodness!

No slugs allowed in the cafeteria!
Now get out of here and put on some socks!

No slugs allowed in the cafeteria!

If anyone in my kingdom is found to be a queen, she shall be taken
up above the world so high
like a gargoyle in the sky.

New Year's Eve Fireworks at the Forks

River and bridge
and things that hover:
      smoke,
      helicopter,
      a nine-year-old girl.

Snow blurs the edges of advancing water,
ripples glowing, thirsty.

The mother searches the sky
for just a flash and

the girl swings leg over rail, straddling
the edge, to look down.

Too innocent to wonder at
      the far of fall,
      the swift of current,
      the gravity of never.

Vasectomy

is a safe and highly effective form
of border control, a virtually painless pro-
hibition of my lifelong plan to become
the Waltons. One snip
seals off the vessels carrying sperm from
your rotting gene pool to mine in late-
night fluid movements, cutting the risk of conceiving
more frightened rabbits than I have hands.
To ensure a severed
marriage is pulled in no more than two
directions, the area is frozen with a prick
of remorse, and then tied or sealed to prevent
culpability for knowingly creating another mouth to
concede. Most men return to their normal life-
style following this minimally
invasive form of permanent
hearth patrol.

(Sic)

they have found autism can be controld by diet it is not a mental condition
tiny sporns (yes like mushroom sporns) that live in the intestine releases
a chemical that affects the brain like alcohol does adults in other words
youre child is drunk this why they loose balance ect Keep a low starch diet
and more protien and watch the diffrence vitamin c or fresh orange juice
helps flush the intestine of the sporn that can never be killed off even with
the strongest antibiodics

—Facebook commenter

To Make an Aspie

Make love to a computer tech beneath a *hoppers ugmart* sign. Line
maternity bras end to end—like digesting cobras—down the hall. For the
first trimester, ingest more than your share of blue food colouring to make
your gut electric. Chant in Klingon. Hang Alpha-getti tins over your bed to
ward off flexibility. Sort your friends by texture: soft ones, set on delicate;
those heavier loads, throw in with the towel. Stuff your pockets with Pop-
Tarts chewed into the shape of pteranodons. Paint your belly with the flags
of uncharted territories. Sleep on annotated maps, the indices to treaties.
Play punk rock (but tell them it was Mozart). Read *What to Expect
When You're Expecting* while hanging upside-down from a laundry list of
excuses. Befriend the last sixty-seven children born without it. Laugh. Feel
the itch and rip out all your labels.

The Imaginative Child Gets a Dog

You can tell a Shepadoodle
from a Labradinger, you pore over pictures
of spays and sutures, you can rate
the heat tolerance of any terrier or hound,
but you won't stop
feeding Lily chocolate chips
under the table to see how long
till she pukes. You say *weird,*
weird, this shepherd-corgi cross
who snubs fruits and veggies,
won't bark or fetch—you suspect
Aspergers. Your brand of torture has
a vaudeville touch: paws shoved into pirate coats,
tutus, and kilts; Lily's brown eyes
beneath your Minnie Mouse ears begging me
for rescue. You hide your head under the covers
when her tongue calls you to breakfast,
push away her kiss goodnight,
but here you are, three a.m., wedged
behind the kennel, fingers laced
between the bars, reaching
for her ear.

Zoo

Italicized words are adapted from the NYU Child Study Centre's "Ransom Notes" campaign and the Autism Speaks "I Am Autism" transcript.

You love that the clownfish can change size, change sex, change colour. Protected by its own sugary coating, it lives under the anemone's toxic sting.

We know where you live.

Wildebeests gather in herds for protection. The antelope who stands out is the one the lions snatch.

We work faster than pediatric AIDS, cancer, and diabetes combined.

Boa constrictors can stretch jaws wide to swallow rabbits whole. You can't wait to show me photos.

We have your son.

Everyone knows cheetahs can outrun us, but that a peregrine falcon can fly 320 kilometres an hour, fly into the sun, fly until he becomes invisible—I know this because of you.

We will make sure he will not be able to care for himself or others for as long as he lives.

Thirty-two acres a minute, you can't stop saying, thirty-two acres of that ape's habitat destroyed, every minute; and you can't see the rest of the primates for your tears.

We are destroying his ability for social interaction and driving him into a life of complete isolation.

Your hand in mine, we watch the hummingbird, with its tongue shaped like a W, lick thirteen times a second, taking in its wishes on wings iridescent as bubbles.

Parents' Weekend Off

1.
We're free to fly the crimson sky, sings Bono.
You crank it up, and in a car with a muffler,
take me back to '92.

We treat Autopac signs like mistletoe;
your forehead presses into mine
at the next light.

2.
It's about time I go seagull hunting, you say
as you take thirty more snapshots
of pests in flight.

They flock to you
while I slide off my bathing strap and
wonder when you'll notice.

3.
Indy finds the Holy Grail. You
bring me chai tea.

We touch each other gingerly
here and here, sages seeking knowledge.
Tracing ruts across ribs.

4.
If our bodies hadn't ached
for more than each other
(sleep, Advil, rebirth as birds), I would

have taken your kiss
to mean more than *goodnight*.

Delayed

He'll be just fine,
you always said,
with love and patience
that boy will come around.
"Aspergers" and "attention deficit"
didn't mean a thing to you. You only saw
a great-grandson's eyes shine
as he climbed onto your bed,
blind to the tubes
that wound their way
to your nose and arm,
binding you to earth
for a little more
time.

Unable to Show Grief

He leans into the casket. There is his granny.

He drops his drawing onto her folded hands.

We stand a moment and stare.

We walk to our seats in the front row.

People watch us.

He does not cry.

> He may be cold.

> He may be strong.

> He may spend the next year running out of the classroom

> for no reason at all.

What Happened after He Coloured Outside the Line

A scream.

He's up.

Don't touch!

I run behind him,

around the sanctuary,

chase him into the basement

class, far from street

exits and frightened ushers and hushed

prayers, I block the door with both arms, scan

for pens, scissors, free-standing shelves, anything

glass, I breathe,

I begin to speak slowly, softly, everything I know

about hovercrafts:

how they float

on a cushion of trapped

air, how they have less footprint

pressure than a one-legged seagull,

how we will build one with a leaf

blower in the garage, how they rescue

people from thin ice and

flood, until he hears and falls to the floor, trembling,

lets me squeeze his shoulders,

stroke his damp hair, until he looks in my eyes

and wants to know: *Why is the chair upside down?*

Why is your arm red?

The Imaginative Child Breaks a Leg

Phone rings, teacher says
you've fallen on your leg: you need
me. I picture you standing at the top
of the slide, crying, *Look at me*,
taking off. Landing well is hard.
I bring the ice and comics, you bring me
to tears. After all the whooping hacks that rang
hollow, bluffed bellyaches, I'm skeptical and
skeptical about my own skepticism.
Receptionist sees swelling.
I'm not sure what I see, but
your wincing as the walk-in doc turns you
at the knee and ankle, requests testing, stirs
my ache. Maybe baby bird's got a broken leg?
The X-ray can't reveal
why you lied about falling.
What shivering need,
what undiagnosable fracture?

For Us

For now
For tomorrow
For cheap
Forewarned
For freedom
For me
For life
Foreplay
For real
For the first time
For a change
For the kitchen
For poorer
For leaks
For the birds
For a song
For nine months
Forceps
For college
For colic
Forbear
For one night
For pity's sake
For depression
Forget it
For Christmas
Four little monkeys
For biting
For funding
For a glass of wine
Forest for the trees
For wrinkles
For kicks
For pancakes
For good

Support Group 2

To those who understand, who can say *encopresis* five times fast and not flinch, who've learned to wait till midnight to bathe with one eye open: let's stick together. Who else knows the side effects of scissors like the backs of their sofas, can rattle off the co-morbid conditions for surrender to Ritalin, the names of three families who cut gluten, the life and death of hardware shopping? We'll share nice and naughty lists of psychiatrists, a torn copy of *House Rules*, anything fragrant and smothered in sauces. We are the calmers of Vesuvius, keepers of routine, defenders of all that is blunt, wordless, unspeakable. We gather in online forums, seeking the verbal. We are the invisible spectacle at every checkout.

III. For Good

But after you've been there for a
while and you catch your breath,
you look around. . . . and
you begin to notice that Holland has windmills . . .
and Holland has tulips.
Holland even has Rembrandts.

this morning you feel a crackle

as if something were about to arrive

the rising smell of yeast

a drizzle   an idling car

packed for a picnic   down the street

a grandpa digs out dusty tools

and a tune   from the past

a daisy that felt the blade reaches up

for warmth   on the refrigerator a kitten

curls up to nap

in the rising smell of the coffee

you're about to enjoy

while your child who cried herself to sleep

begins to sing

The Diminutive Professor Has a Party

What would happen if we probed Proxima Centauri? he asks as I spill a
pitcher of "Yoda soda" on the gluten-free wieners.

He holds up his design, a sports car of a spacecraft, made entirely of
programmable matter. *How many ion engines would it need to break the
atmosphere?* he wants to know. I can barely keep track of eight kazoos.

I greet the first mother at the gate, while the voice beside my hip explains
the repulsor field. *Ion drives are a good source of propulsion*, he tells me;
They start out slow but keep accelerating forever. He charts Andromeda,
orbits bewildered classmates.

As I tie the Death Star piñata into the apple tree, I ask him, *So how many
Twizzlers does it take to reach the moon? One*, he says, *if it's long enough.*

Autism for Dummies 3

1.
weather reports from the autism front
the sound of falling snow
a rainbow over my house
      pre-Rain Man

alone together
now I see the moon

what colour is Monday

2.
more than hope
just give him the whale

the out-of-sync child has fun
emerging from the bonds
hot pink and zebra striped

the best kind of different
unleashing
songs of the gorilla nation

Mozart knocks autism on its ear

      girl with kaleidoscope eyes
      strange son
your greatness is growing

sometimes it's all about the cream cheese

look me in the eye
      you're going to love this kid

The Imaginative Child Aces Grade Three Math

Under your desk, palms white-glued together like you're praying
for a break—peel-peel-peeling off sticky strings
feels so good. Feet slip-slop in those crocs
to the boys' bathroom to see if you'll get caught, then skip
off to google skateboarding dogs in sunglasses
when you should be discovering the Northwest Passage
to math class. From the library, your new glasses, wedged
between Nancy Drew and Ogopogo, see everything.
Hey hon, why ya hiding under your chair
meowing? Sure, cats don't do math, but you're good
at multiplying: six stern looks by ten o'clock.
Hear the bell, bolt for the door, and count:
the boot rack caught your seven flying socks and
three muddy mitts this week. For homework: list ten
reasons not to moon the teacher.

Butterflies

In the photo,
she is smiling.
Not for the camera,

but for her dad behind it.
She smiles past a hundred
unreadable faces.

Click.

She flits
down dark stage steps,
over tight rows of toes

to light on Daddy's lap,
while the rest of the elves
sing on.

This is the picture
the mother—still holding
the girl's wet tissues
in the gym doorway—takes home:

her head resting on his shoulder,
arms wrapped tight
as ribbon.

Support Group 3

Oh my God oh my God oh my God! Tracy's mom flaps her hands over
our doughnuts like a priest on speed because she R-R-Rolled Up the Rim
to Win a coffee, beside Brady's mom who doesn't look up from picking
her peeling cuticles and staring at the crystal lamp she lost on eBay—*the
one that sparkled!*—while Cody's mom grimaces at Katie's mom and
her looping story of the dog that's been missing since 1982. From the
screaming orange walls, *Hit me baby one more time!* jabs my ribs apart
and I curl up inside like a night crawler in a sunbeam. We know every line
in *Pride and Prejudice.* We collect *Bazinga!* shirts and badass bows. We
laugh at farts and cry at yard sales. We agree our kids take after their silent
fathers. We steer clear of crowds and wool.

Pillow Talk

My husband and I talk about the same things you do. Safe things, like the leaning fence and the brakes about to give out. Why he leaves his socks under the coffee table. What to do about the dog vomiting on the carpet. Where we left our earplugs.

We talk about the past. Is he getting too burned out again to hold his job. Will he slip back under the covers, shades drawn, and charge me with the full-time job of shushing. Will we have to choose between food and private school. How would we survive without lattes.

We talk about the future. If we can't keep our daughter from breaking into my locked makeup drawer, if we can't stop her from saying *gross!* to tattooed thugs, if a man asks to see her breasts, if the funding runs out, if they run away, if they live with us forever.

Some nights, too tired for words, we type to each other from separate rooms. *Did you eat the last grapefruit? Have we already watched "The Survivor in the Soap"? When are you coming to bed?*

Campground Shower

A smell of swamp water,
imprint of crab and leech,
crust of sand and weed
on your small, stretched suit,
your matted hair beneath my chin
as we cool our flaming shoulders,
wash Band-Aids down the drain.
Tilt toward me
while I run my fingers
through your tangles,
rinse bugs and suds and
watch water fall
over your grape-skin bum,
imaginary buds,
the white lines
that cross your back,
marking a treasure
or a target.

Camping

I will write a poem about today before
today is lost forever. It will recall the fire that drew us,
the trees that kept us, the chickadees and squirrels
dropping in to register their approval,
the cookies passed around,
the way nobody said or did
anything worth remembering.
Perfect.

The Imaginative Child Storms the Beach

You've gathered quite the following, kindred
spirits fearless in the face of slimy weeds
and dangling leeches. Armed
with a pink butterfly net and pail, you stalk
the reeds for anything that leaps: a frog, a toad,
an alligator. The baby crayfish, no longer than your chewed
pinky nail, was surprised when you pinched
first. You release the moths from the jar, and
now there's room for six, no seven, no eight spotted leeches,
refusing to pop under pressure.
While your admirers gape, you lift a pollywog
to your lips and, with one kiss, turn yourself
into a dolphin and swim away.

Corporophobia: the Fear of Strange Toilets

After seven years of your screams
streaming past cracked mirrors, your flushed
face drowning in its own imagination,
flooded yellow rooms reflected
in your pooling eyes,

this morning, with one finger,
you press the lever down
two inches below your fear,
exit the campground stall
with a triumphant *ha!*
and wash your hands of the whole mess,

your glistening palms
meeting mine with a clap
loud enough to spook our demons,
send them swirling down.

Taste and See

My first Saskatoon pie bubbles over in my oven-mitted arms.

The berries grew along our path to St. Malo beach, where my daughter mixed a seaweed cure for sadness.

St. Malo means "beautiful captive."

As I filled my pail, she peppered me with good news: a painted turtle by the bathroom, a swallow's nest, baby bunnies under that bush.

My thoughts rose to the sheltering oaks and the falcon circling. I will never hear what moves it.

The camper before us backed over a pine sapling. My son dug it out to nurse to health outside his window.

Some of the berries grew so deep in poison ivy that only the deer and her fawn could reach them. They looked at me, but I didn't understand the question.

Every year, my son's pine will grow three inches.

The rain falls like a word. Then a story, soaking in.

I left the mountain of wet beach towels and dusty sheets in our entrance to wash my berries, preheat the oven.

My daughter is at the piano, hymnal open, singing *as long as Thou lendest me breath* to her own tune.

The berries rush to fill the gap my first slice leaves behind.

In winter, almost all of our tiny pine will be invisible. Except the crown, pointing up.

A camp counsellor once told me the Trinity is like a pie: three equal pieces, one fluid filling.

Sweet juice traces a path to my chin. Repurples my tongue.

Faith

I am not like Jacob: I
had no twin to wrap my arm
around as we slept. No nightly
angels climb down my darkened
stare or dance under my pin as I
dream on this lonely, God-forsaken rock.

But I too have fought through blackness,
groping for the twisting arm of
a strangeness that won't let go before
it blesses me. I too have grasped
a nearness that ached to slip me
out of joint, wrest from me old names,
old ways of limping.

The Diminutive Professor Stays Close

At edges, at crossings,
at twelve, dear boy, your hand
reaches for mine
and doesn't let go
until we come to a door
where my fingers
will slip from our knot
to recover a set of keys,
your misplaced jacket,
that just-me sensation.
Interlocked, we walk
snug as two halves
of your hoodie.

Self-assured boy-men
wearing skulls on their sleeves
(whose mothers, left holding
Buzz Lightyear boots,
have faded)
pass and stare
at our blatant affection,
our zippered selves,
our innocent rebellion.

Posthumously Diagnosed

Michelangelo slept in his clothes and seldom ate   Newton lectured
to empty rooms at scheduled times even if no one showed up to hear
him   At five Mozart composed a minuet   A man of few words in a
three-cornered hat and faded velvet, Cavendish discovered inflammable air,
always ate mutton   Napoleon made his servants break in his boots   Only
staying where room numbers were divisible by three, Tesla tested turbines
in his mind, would not touch round objects   After hearing it once,
Mozart set down the score of *Miserere* from memory   Jim Henson
gave our inner Cookie Monsters and Kermits free rein   Einstein rarely
thought in words, had hair like yours   Andy Warhol drank Campbell's
soup for lunch for twenty years   Mozart wrote six hundred masterpieces
by age thirty-five   Prone to tantrums, Hans Christian Andersen told
emperors the naked truth, expounded on the pain of a single pea, believed
in swans   Charles Darwin formulated the theory of natural selection,
the foundation for our understanding of the diversity of life on
earth: advantageous traits survive   Mozart meowed on tables

Fortune Cookies

You have the instinct to care for those around you.

      Today someone will not let you hug her.

You yearn for success but will settle for safe passage through parking lots.

      You will be covered in butter. And blame. And bubbles.

Your judgment is off. Rely on those closest to you.

      Look for loved ones under clothing racks. With your fly down.

God never opens more doors than you have handles.

      You're braver than your mother-in-law ever imagined.

Soon someone will make you very proud.

My Front Row Seat

Why didn't you warn me there was something very wrong with your son? —kindergarten teacher

In Dad's tie, hair slicked, you stand taller

than fear, take centre stage, shoulder to shoulder

with boys you can name and girls

you may or may not have noticed

yet—your eighth-grade teacher gives you the thumbs up

and voices from our past pile up inside me

(the worst case ... not able ... no reason to believe

... locked room where he'll be safe),

but thin words can't fill my mind

like your eyes meeting mine:

you wink and say

your first line

Echolalia (the Sibling Rivalry)

This day we fight!
By all that you hold dear on this good earth,
I bid you stand, men of the West!

Did you notice I was holding a banana?

Expelliarmus!

How dare you hit me with a giant medieval flail!

Beware the eyes of March!

Expelapillow! Expelapillow!

I see in your eyes the same fear that would take the heart of me!

Cloaking device!

Red hair, hand-me-down robe, you must be a Weasley.

Expelapickle! Expelapickle!

Besides you're saying it wrong. It's Leviosa, not Leviosar!

I will rule the Tri-State area. Behold my mustache-inator!

Romeo, Romeo, let down your hair!

Wherefore art thou, Romulan?

You will be assimilated.

If Baggins loses, we eats it whole.

I Choose You

Do you remember how you called my cat Tristan your *nasal mist*? Remember those ugly matching Smurf shirts Mom sewed us, so she couldn't lose us in public? The Christmas I gave you chicken pox?

Remember the way I risked my life on the swing set to put on a circus for you? The day you could have crashed the El Camino into Oma's kitchen, but I didn't stop you in case something interesting finally happened to us?

The way we kept *A Small World* spinning? My *Go, go, go!* when you won the relay. The number of times we had to knock the punching clown, orbit the dehumidifier, and land on the Rebounder to be crowned king. Our victory song.

How you beamed when you got your first lawnmower and gave me your business card. The way you kissed your fingers like an Italian chef when you fried me perogies.

The night a man in a dream asked if I'd trade you for a puppy and I said yes, the way I cried myself awake because I missed you.

Support Group 4

Home, we three are
bag lunches, clogged sinks,
left turns,

wounded foxes—claws
retracting.

Here at this cabin, we transform
into vessels for wine,
brie, and story.

Settling into easy
chairs, our feet sheathed
in slippers,

we rise
only to fill
each other's glasses,

catch a glimpse of
raven wing.

Unwary, we doze off
in dens of fleece.

This Eucharist of
broken chocolate
sustains us.

To Make a More Imperfect Person

Teach me to yell like a Wookie, yodel like hell. Gone are the days of overthinking the Cat in the Hat's motivation. No more wearing white. Wild child, give your mother words for all that's alien: hyperdrives, holodecks, and naps. Make me forget the names of acid-washed bullies and the reason I ever leave the room. Teach me that four p.m. is made for Froot Loops and disco. Burp the Greek alphabet to the tune of Zest commercials. Let's reclaim Narnia for the Naiads while the rigatoni burns. Who says it's rude to praise shoppers for their resemblance to stegosauri? Oh baby, make me toss the experts; make me believe in mutants and mermaids again. When I see dust, show me sparkle. Grant me earworms and wormholes, earthworms and whims. Write me a thesaurus in which the synonym for *soothe* is *keep your distance* and the opposite of *late* is *just stay home*. Smear my smug chin with peanut butter. Teach me to hide mother's little helpers (Dr. Pepper and 3 Musketeers) in the folded arms of sweaters. Make me choose between losing you at Value Village and starring as your abductor on Canada AM. See me hang loose like my emptied junk drawer—ready for anything.

Anything Besides

I will write about something—anything—besides
this

because my heart can't take
one more child blistering in shitty pants
because schools are busy teaching other children to
count,

one more breaking
story about a child wandering off
to drown in a ditch
fifty feet from home.

I can't spend one more moment on regret
over the expert advice I should have ignored
the nights I wept outside your door
as I held it shut,

one more moment of rage
over everything they shouldn't have said:
*But he looks so normal. She just needs a good
spanking. Have you tried
enemas? I don't know
how you do it.*

It—by which they mean
get out of bed. As if
they haven't considered
the alternative.

I won't repeat
how tired I am of hearing
that vegan cheese will
change everything.

The Imaginative Child Goes to Bed

Catwoman, Queen of Hearts, Medusa—each time I pass your door, there's a different villain in another cape—Vader's line of evening gowns pulled tight around your ribs. Your cheeks blush with Cover Girl charm stolen from my drawers. I moan and beg you into bed, but can't compete with your reflection as you whirl yourself into a leading lady. Aha, I see what you're hiding under that pillow: screwdriver, eyeliner, permanent pen. Can't sleep, hon? Fine, just one more massage with lavender cream, one more drink of water, one more trip to the bathroom to see if you've grown breasts. Midnight. At last your lair is still, save "Born This Way" blaring from beneath your discarded bears. I ballet step over your snug-as-a-bun roll, red heels and wig spilling from the ends like ketchup. Chocolate wrappers clog your vent, sweetening the air. I reach for the off button. Above your dresser, happy faces etched into drywall smile back at me, dreamily, and wink.

confession

I don't pray much
my words too blunt to pierce a divine ear
my thoughts too heavy to fly
in the face of gravity
I don't pray much
      unless you count the reaching
and resigning of my breast
seventeen thousand times a day
the testing
and trusting under my feet
in every forward, backward
place
      the way my eyelids close
to the mess I cannot clear
I make chaos disappear
and in the morning dare to rise
                 again

And the pain of that
will never, ever, ever, ever
go away . . .
because the loss of that dream
is a very very significant loss.
But . . . if you spend your life
mourning the fact that you didn't get
to Italy, you may never be
free to enjoy the very special,
the very lovely things
. . . about Holland.

NOTES

"Delayed" is in memory of my grandma Margaret Froese (Mar. 20, 1922–Jan. 31, 2009). "Waving" is for Mona. "The Runaway Housewife at One a.m." is for Jennifer. "Watching Him Sleep 1" is for Edith. "Beyond Words" is for Therese. "Support Group 3" is for Crystal and Ruby. "Support Group 4" is for Shellie and Elona.

Some lines in "Echolalia (the Sibling's Dialogue)" are taken from Focus on the Family's *Adventures in Odyssey* stories. Some lines in "Echolalia (the Monologue)" are from *Robot Zot* by Jon Scieszka. Lines in "Echolalia (the Sibling Rivalry)" are from everywhere geeks live.

Italicized lyrics in "The Diminutive Professor Visits the Duck Pond" are from "Here by the Water," recorded by Steve Bell and written by Jim Croegaert. Copyright 1986, Rough Stones Music (RoughStonesMusic. com), 827 Monroe St., Evanston, IL 60202, USA. All rights reserved. Used by permission.

"Autism for Dummies" is a series of found poems created from autism book titles.

The book referenced in "What Doctors Took Seven Years to Discover" is *Amazingly . . . Alphie: Understanding and Accepting Different Ways of Being* by Roz Espin.

"Building Blocks of Attachment" was a program run by the Child Development Clinic, Winnipeg.

"You Must Believe in Life after Yesterday" is after Jan Zwicky's "You Must Believe in Spring"; "Support Group 2," after Sue Goyette's "Lost"; "Waving," after Don McKay's "Antler."

"DSM-5: Aphorism Speculum Disorder (ASD)" is a modified Oulipo n+7, in which nearby words from the dictionary begin replacing the originals.

"(Sic)" appeared in a comment on Jim Walter's Facebook post about taking his daughter to Target and was reposted in "Flush the Sporns!" on JustaLilBlog.com, Sept. 12, 2012. Used by permission.

"We come to land," "hen you're going to have a baby cat," "The important thing is that they haven't taken a rib," "But after," and "And the hat" are erasures of "Welcome to Holland" by Emily Perl Kingsley, the text many mothers receive from friends after their child is diagnosed with a disability.

Welcome To Holland
by Emily Perl Kingsley

©1987 by Emily Perl Kingsley. All rights reserved.
Reprinted by permission of the author.

I am often asked to describe the experience of raising a child with a disability—to try to help people who have not shared that unique experience to understand it, to imagine how it would feel. It's like this......

When you're going to have a baby, it's like planning a fabulous vacation trip—to Italy. You buy a bunch of guide books and make your wonderful plans. The Coliseum. The Michelangelo David. The gondolas in Venice. You may learn some handy phrases in Italian. It's all very exciting.

After months of eager anticipation, the day finally arrives. You pack your bags and off you go. Several hours later, the plane lands. The flight attendant comes in and says, "Welcome to Holland."

"Holland?!?" you say. "What do you mean Holland?? I signed up for Italy! I'm supposed to be in Italy. All my life I've dreamed of going to Italy."

But there's been a change in the flight plan. They've landed in Holland and there you must stay.

The important thing is that they haven't taken you to a horrible, disgusting, filthy place, full of pestilence, famine and disease. It's just a different place.

So you must go out and buy new guide books. And you must learn a whole new language. And you will meet a whole new group of people you would never have met.

It's just a <u>different</u> place. It's slower-paced than Italy, less flashy than Italy. But after you've been there for a while and you catch your breath, you look around. . . . and you begin to notice that Holland has windmills. . . . and Holland has tulips. Holland even has Rembrandts.

But everyone you know is busy coming and going from Italy . . . and they're all bragging about what a wonderful time they had there. And for the rest of your life, you will say "Yes, that's where I was supposed to go. That's what I had planned."

And the pain of that will never, ever, ever, ever go away . . . because the loss of that dream is a very very significant loss.

But . . . if you spend your life mourning the fact that you didn't get to Italy, you may never be free to enjoy the very special, the very lovely things . . . about Holland.

THANK YOU

To Méira Cook, my mentor in the Manitoba Writers' Guild Sheldon Oberman Mentorship Program, for good beginnings . . . and a little luck.

To my editor Alayna Munce for her attention to detail, and for giving me a sock reference quota. To Barry Dempster for appreciating my "guts," to Marijke Friesen for the beautiful cover, to Sue Sinclair for the careful copy edits, and to Kitty Lewis for being awesome.

To the 2013 Sage Hill Poetry Colloquium: instructor Don McKay, E.D. Philip Adams, and "sage ones" Kimmy Beach, dee Hobsbawn-Smith, Madhur Anand, Katia Grubisic, Kathleen Wall, Kevin Spenst, Henry Rappaport, and Heidi Garnett.

To the other poets who have workshopped these poems, most recently Sue Wonnek, Melanie Dennis Unrau, Kate Grisim, Jennifer Still, Luann Hiebert, Sally Ito, Sarah Klassen, Gregory Scofield, Erín Moure, Roo Borson, Di Brandt, and the members of the May Day Poetry Project. And especially Joanne Epp, who has been there from the beginning.

To Annemarie Wiebe and Ernie Braun, the first teachers who pointed me toward poetry.

To the Manitoba Writers' Guild, Thin Air, Speaking Crow, and McNally Robinson Booksellers for making Winnipeg a great place to write.

To my family at Crossroads MB Church and Hope Centre Ministries for prayers and belonging.

To my parents for their support and to my in-laws for their joy in my work. To Chad and Tim for making me a compassionate sister. To my husband Tony for his friendship through the crazy years. And to my fabulous children: I will never wash my hands of this weirdness.

To the editors of the following publications, in which earlier versions of some of these poems appeared: *Prairie Fire, CV2, Rejoice!, The New Quarterly, Geez, Rhubarb, Room, The Society*, the *MB Herald*, the Envoi Festival website, Wordgathering.com, Leaf Press's *Cradle Song* anthology and *Leaflet* series. Versions of some poems have also appeared in the chapbook *Roads of Stone* (Alfred Gustav Press, Series Fourteen).

To the Manitoba Arts Council and the Sage Hill Writing Experience for financial support during the creation of this manuscript.

ANGELINE SCHELLENBERG's poems have appeared in journals such as *CV2*, *TNQ*, *Grain*, and *Lemon Hound*. Her first chapbook, *Roads of Stone* (the Alfred Gustav Press), launched in May 2015. Her poetry won third prize in *Prairie Fire*'s 2014 Banff Centre Bliss Carman Poetry Award Contest and was shortlisted for *Arc Poetry Magazine*'s 2015 Poem of the Year. Angeline lives and reads in Winnipeg with her husband, their two teenagers, and a German shepherd-corgi.